67
MIXED MESSAGES

ahsahta press

The New Series

number 12

67 MIXED MESSAGES

POEMS BY ED ALLEN

AHSAHTA PRESS

Boise State University • Boise • Idaho • 2006

Ahsahta Press, Boise State University
Boise, Idaho 83725
http://ahsahtapress.boisestate.edu

Copyright © 2006 by Ed Allen
Printed in the United States of America
Cover art by Grant Olsen
Author photograph by Laura Wehde
Book and cover design by Janet Holmes
First printing January 2006
ISBN 0-916272-86-9

Library of Congress Cataloging-in-Publication Data

Allen, Edward, 1948-
    67 mixed messages : poems / by Ed Allen.
      p. cm. -- (The new series ; no. 12)
    ISBN 0-916272-86-9 (pbk. : alk. paper)
    1. Sonnets, American. 2. Women college students--Poetry. 3. Bisexuality--Poetry. I. Title.
II. Title: Sixty-seven mixed messages. III. Series: New series (Ahsahta Press) ; no. 12.
    PS3551.L39225A614 2006
    811'.54--dc22
                                2005011475

ACKNOWLEDGMENTS

Poems #1, "Suzi on a Windy Day," and #47, "Some Linguistic Theories," were published in *Indiana Review*.

Poem #3, "Suzi Dancing Alone in Overalls," and poem #4 appeared in *Seattle Review*.

Whose love is given over-well
Shall look on Helen's face in hell
Whilst they whose love is thin and wise
Shall see John Knox in Paradise.

—Dorothy Parker

Contents

PART ONE

1	Suzi on a Windy Day	3
2	In a College Bar	4
3	Suzi Dancing Alone in Overalls	5
4		6
5	When Did I Last Touch Suzi?	7
6	An Offering of Shoes	8
7	Listening to Lonnie Mack's Song "Satisfy Suzy"	9
8	Figuring Out Lines Based on a Name	10
9		11
10	Some Hopes of Traveling	12
11	What It Would Be Like to Hold Hands with Suzi	13
12	What It Would Be Like to Be One of Suzi's Boyfriends	14
13	What It Would Be Like to Have Suzi Looking up into My Eyes the Way Actresses Do in Porno Movies	15
14		16
15	In Criminal Justice Class	17
16	How Would I Feel if Suzi Killed Somebody?	18
17		19
18		20
19	Her Bathroom Mirror	21
20	Imagining Suzi on the School Bus	22
21	What It's Like to Be Made Unhappy	23
22	What Two Guys in the Pub Said	24

PART TWO

23		27
24		28
25		29
26		30
27		31
28	Thoughts on a Traveling Day	32
29		33
30	Thoughts While at a Conference	34
31		35
32		36
33	Is It Appropriate to Indulge these Fantasies?	37
34	Suzi as a Literary Object	38
35		39
36		40
37		41
38		42
39	The Fact That She is Less Than Half My Age	43
40		44
41	Suzi Disguised as a Body Pillow	45
42	On the Campus Walkway	46
43	Suzi Drinking Soda on a Hot Day	47
44		48
45		49
46	Suzi as a Nonexistent Person	50
47	Some Linguistic Theories	51
48	An Apologetically Sexist Meditation in Time of War	52
49	Her Possible Fiancé	53

PART THREE

50	The Difference Between Suzi's Boyfriends and Me	57
51	Suzi Tells a Lie	58
52		59
53		60
54		61
55	Suzi Smoking	62
56		63
57		64
58	How Can I Adjust a Debt and Not Make Suzi Look Bad?	65
59	Suzi Getting Ready for the State Beauty Pageant	66
60	Fall Colors, Beauty Pageant	67
61		68
62		69
63	On the Day of the University Parade	70
64	Thinking about Suzi on a Day When I Don't Have Any Desire For Her	71
65	In a College Bar on Halloween	72
66	Watching Suzi Pull Out of my Driveway	73
67	Watching Suzi Drive Away on a Day When She Looks Heavier	74

PART ONE

1

Suzi on a Windy Day

Into the all-day gust she turns her head,
Letting the long horizon make a blur
Of land and houses, trees alive and dead,
Vanishing with the earth's slow curvature—
Except the towns get meaner to the west:
She said one kid from school, called "Fag Boy," died
Upended in a Dumpster, hunting vest
Zipped tight across his face; ruled suicide.

I love you, Suzi. Though the wind shakes glass,
Great things can happen in a state this bare.
Ramshackle trailers of the student class
Are small panoptica of earth and air,
Centered so that each rattling window frame
Enfolds the Tetragram that has no name.

2

In a College Bar

Impassive, blank, unsmiling, Suzi's one
Loose-trousered nameless friend slumps in the seat,
Orders that scab-brewed beer, then starts to run
Vague hands in Suzi's hair, to Green Day's beat.
Everyone knows me here, so no gay jokes.
She holds his hard male gaze, a focused stare.
Up at the bar she buys a pack of smokes.
Zippos are flicked at once from everywhere.

I love you Suzi. Let me fit someplace,
Get better beer for you than will this friend.
Reptiles stalk prey with stares like that guy's face,
And note—such men laugh less each year: a trend.
"Coors Light," he orders, for the drunk drive home,
Ending with you. (I hope it comes out foam.)

Suzi Dancing Alone in Overalls

In Lou's, where they don't like me, she was there,
Loaded, I'm sure, wearing her "overhauls,"
Old, frayed, no doubt a Civic Council pair,
Vertical stripes, nothing you'd find in malls.
Everyone saw how still she held her face.
Some girls can dance and not know where they are,
Untouched by school and all its paper chase,
Zen-faced, in overhauls, drunk in a bar.

I love you, Suzi, how your denim bib
Girdles your soft breasts as you hold your face
Rapt with the motion, while your feet ad lib,
And still John Mellencamp rings through the place.
Concubines draped in silk have never been
Equal to how that coarse weave smoothes your skin.

4

It's great to see her in her "overhauls,"
Looking at once a model and a hick,
Old-fashioned cut, but one that Glamour calls
"Viagra: even gays will want this chick."
Elastic holds her shoulder strap in place,
Slung like the weasel in an old cartoon.
Up from the denim bib, I see her face,
Zoned on John Mellencamp, that rich baboon.

I love you, Suzi, wild in dungarees,
Grace in the barnyard, denim touching skin,
Rugged strong fabric, with a chain of keys,
As if each night you locked the chickens in.
Cotton is cool, and Suzi brings this town
Excitement in a Goodwill hand-me-down.

When Did I Last Touch Suzi?

It might have been the time she shook her hair
Loosely in front of me in Lou's dark loft.
Or did she idly run her fingers there:
Veiled bid for me to come and feel how soft?
Each time we've had a drink there's been someone
Sitting there with us, so I couldn't speak
Until I had to make a bathroom run,
Zigzagging through the crowd to take a leak.

I love you, Suzi. Dreams of you with me
Go on for hours at home; I sit awake,
Rereading Roethke's lines—coming, you'll see,
A mile behind you for your pretty sake.
Come winter, maybe, when the ground is white,
End of semester, we can touch all night.

6

An Offering of Shoes

I'd like to see her walking in high heels,
Looking at me, pretending I'm all right,
On our first date (those May–December deals),
Vanilla skin, pale, painted, in the night.
Each compass point shows women, calves pulled straight,
Smooth balanced, their whole body on a stage,
Up off the flat ground, lifted from their weight,
Zen-like, a text above the earth's blank page.

I love you, Suzi. Pick what brand you choose:
Gas-cushioned Nikes, slippers trimmed in pearl,
Round-toed Doc Marten's, wooden platform shoes,
And sharp-heeled "fuck boots" like a working girl.
Come with me, Suzi, you can be my most
Expensive girlfriend on the Middle Coast.

Listening to Lonnie Mack's Song "Satisfy Suzy"

In songs like what I have on this CD,
Loud rocker Lonnie Mack savors the name
Of Suzi, though he spells it differently;
(V-bodied Gibson makes all songs the same).
Escaping traffic, Lonnie knows he must
Satisfy Suzi, Pontiac huge-finned,
Under a sky that kicks up swirls of dust,
Zooms in on Suzi's hair stirred by the wind.

I love you, Suzi. What a sweetly dressed
Girlfriend you'd be, for some more normal guy,
Right here, my Escort's tank filled with high-test,
As wind in motion makes the dustballs fly.
Cut more tracks, Lon, for Suzi is a wild,
Exciting girl with front-seat hair wind-styled.

8

Figuring Out Lines Based on a Name

It's fun to puzzle through the alphabet
Looking for words that catch her as she is.
Obscure or plain, they constitute a set:
Verse, chapter, canto, like a midterm quiz.
Ending a day is hard without her voice,
Sky rainless, fevered; farmers struck by drought.
Until my Y genes turn me straight, this choice
Zip code we live in's just a paper route.

I love you, Suzi. Metaphors of rain
Go barely halfway to describe the dark
Riverbed of your eyes, shaped from the plain
Acrostic where I've spelled your name in stark
Columns, arranged like faces in a choir,
Each line, for Suzi, straight as mason's wire.

9

If all girls were like Suzi, life would be
Like New Year's in the Castro, but there's just
One Suzi for each world, and none for me,
Valves of attention closed, as stone valves must.
Each time she takes her dress off by her bed,
Stripped down to bra and panties (man, this hurts),
Until she parts the covers with her head,
Zen-like, her breath comes out in Yogic spurts.

I love you Suzi, though your darting tongue
Gives joy only to others and your hair
Rests on the pillow of some guy who's hung
A bedside trophy of your underwear.
Call off the dreaming. Suzi's far away.
Envy's a bore this early in the day.

10

Some Hopes of Traveling

Into the zone above, the thin flyway,
Leaving the clumps of turbulence below,
On top of scattered cumulus, we may
Vow in the air, mile high, to let things flow.
Even if not, I still mean what I've said:
Some time before I'm gone, that we'll sit tall,
Up near the rain-shaft of a thunderhead,
Zooming along—it's still warm after all.

I love you, Suzi. Think of all the air
Growing around us, and the airport lights
Ringed with a rainbow border everywhere,
And soft with kerosene on summer nights.
Come fly with me, let's fly, let's make this trip.
Ed knows a chapel on the Vegas Strip.

11

What It Would Be Like to Hold Hands with Suzi

In soft light, in the mall, I want to go,
Leaving the lot that overlooks three states,
On floors that let foot traffic smoothly flow,
Variety of colors, heights, and weights.
Each couple holding hands does it the same:
She with her left hand, forward-facing palm,
Up to the white block type of Sears's name,
Zigzagging to avoid some child-stalled mom.

I love you, Suzi: let me hold your hand.
Give me that something: Lennon said it best,
Rhythmically loud: "I think you'll understand."
And when I touch you, warm air fills my chest,
Calms all the clutter of a shopping day,
Erased, like food-court spillings wiped away.

12

What It Would Be Like to Be One of Suzi's Boyfriends

I'm making things much worse; the dream's gone stale.
(Let's dream it anyway): Suzi in bed,
On K-Mart sheets, hair spread out on percale.
Viewed in the light, it shows a dash of red.
Each time I touch her, she comes more alive.
She "lets me know she's there," quick as a spark;
Under the covers, takes a deep sea dive,
Zephyrs of warm breath in the heated dark.

I love you, Suzi. If you read this, please
Grant me one night to learn why straight men care.
Rest with me afterward, in pillowed ease,
A Winston's smoke-trail rising in the air.
Copy these dreams on paper; I'll be back,
Exiled at home, like Boris Pasternak.

13

What It Would Be Like to Have Suzi Looking up into My Eyes the Way Actresses Do in Porno Movies

It would be good; that much at least I'm sure:
Lounging together in a private place
One cheek soft in the dim light's curvature,
Vacantly staring up into my face.
Each time I look at her, her soft eyes blink—
Spherical bodies wider than the moon—
Until she says, "You've had too much to drink."
Zones shift, as in a Japanese cartoon.

I love you, Suzi. Let me, some bright day,
Gaze downward at your sweet face being kind,
Resting in warmth, your soft skin smooth as clay,
Although thus far the film's just in my mind:
Collected Dreams of Suzi, Triple X—
Even the ticket clerks will crane their necks.

14

If I've been on vacation, she's been home,
Leaning on cushions, watching *Jeopardy!*
On mornings when she works out at the Dome,
Varsity lifters watch her hungrily.
End of the summer; everyone should get
Some time for travel: water, land or air.
Under her trailer roof, I can just bet
Zeroed-out credit cards have kept her there.

I love you, Suzi, and I have a dream—
Great God Almighty—that we shall be free,
Released into Las Vegas, where I seem
Abruptly to be saying, "Marry me."
Chapels flash light all down the Boulevard.
Electric bells all tell me, "Play this card."

15

In Criminal Justice Class

I've never seen her in a class, her head
Languidly tilted, brown hair hanging soft.
One case study: a kid whose folks were dead
Viciously killed a man because he coughed.
Each crime is different; perpetrators take
Some tests that show they wouldn't hurt a fly.
Under the tycoon's yacht they dragged the lake,
Zipped up the body bag and then stood by.

I love you, Suzi. Strange to think of you
Going to class where cruelty is the text.
Rape, homicide, the things that people do
Are awful, and you never know who's next.
Crime seems so weird, though if you said to me,
"Erase that guy," he would be history.

16

How Would I Feel if Suzi Killed Somebody?

If Suzi were a felon—even then,
Locked up in jail, I'm sure I'd love her still,
On Sundays visiting with other men,
Vowing to marry even one who'd kill.
Even if Suzi robbed a grocery store,
Slew seven customers, and got away
Un-penitent, I'd love her even more,
Zapata-like, raiding the banks each day.

I love you, Suzi. I can't name a crime
Grotesque enough to make your sweet face stop
Running across my thoughts; if you did time,
All year I'd wince each time I saw a cop.
Cellblocks can't cramp her, Gary Gilmore style.
Elfin, she says, "Let's do it," with a smile.

17

I don't remember what it is she drives—
LeBaron, something, I'm not really sure.
Old cars come here to finish out their lives,
Valves leaking, transportation of the poor.
Enough of that—Suzi deserves to own
Something to make them point as she goes by:
Up in the high end, black Nokia phone
Zips past, in PT Cruiser, on the fly.

I love you, Suzi, and someday I will
Give you a birthday ribbon, shiny blue,
Running from bed, through kitchen, down the hill,
And there stands Suzi's shining . . . Subaru!
Cold cylinders warm up, we're set to steer
East to the towns where Genesee's the beer.

18

Ivy Estates, a shady, quiet spot:
Lane 6, a two-tone metal singlewide.
On just the tenth part of an acre lot,
Veiled by tall shrubs, where kids from next door hide.
Each window shows her face, I'd like to think.
She lives here, waits for this term's Stafford check.
Under the floor, no skirting, leaky sink,
Zigzagging winds beneath the plywood deck.

I love you, Suzi, sweet face framed in steel,
Going from door to window, as the sound
Rises through cracks—I know how that must feel:
A floor that shakes, a room that moves around.
Come to the kitchen window, show your eyes
Edged by sheet metal, as the daylight dies.

19

Her Bathroom Mirror

In humid light, the texture of her face
Lies softly in its second coat, her eyes
Outlined, with lashes dark against the base,
Vanilla cream touched on until it dries.
Expert shade-blending elevates each cheek
So that she's Marlene Dietrich on the screen.
Up higher still, both eyes are touched with sleek
Zinc tracings in an iridescent green.

I love you, Suzi. What if I had just
Gone off to beauty school? By now I'd be
Rewarded for my skill, as artists must,
An expert versed in cosmetology,
Contouring with a brush your soft black eyes,
Egged on alone—or does this thrill most guys?

20

Imagining Suzi on the School Bus

In half-light, shaded, I can almost see
Long bus rides home from school, with boys whose genes
One day would make them turn out just like me:
Victim of that huge secret through their teens.
Embarrassed once in music class, face red,
Shyly, she hid her eyes behind her hand.
Up at the desk in front the teacher said,
"Zithers and lutes are cousins in the band."

I love you, Suzi, how a small child's eyes
Grew dark over eight years, till, dazed with love,
Relations gushed, "She's Bernhardt in disguise!"
And stroked your hair, with hands I'm jealous of,
Collected icebox pictures that you drew:
Each day one more. (My parents lost mine too.)

21

What It's Like to Be Made Unhappy

It even hurts when she's just sitting there,
Lying that I'd slept with a boy—but then,
On balance, does one woman anywhere,
Vermillion, Sioux Falls, give this much to men?
Each time she talks about her boyfriend's wheels,
Something inside me rears, a horse's mane.
Unkindness, when it comes from Suzi, feels
Zones far removed from what I know as pain.

I love you, Suzi. You can be as bad,
Greedy, promiscuous, dishonest, blind.
Remember that the times you make me sad
Are just like Cindy Crawford being kind,
Catching me with that pain, as if she'd swung
Extensions of her hair so hard it stung.

22

What Two Guys in the Pub Said

It made me prick my ears up in my stall,
Learning these things, which I already knew.
One guy said she'd been out with nearly all
Vermillion, and the other said, "That's true."
Ears hear so much, despite the barroom noise;
Secrets don't keep, even with voice held low.
"Under the covers, Suzi's nice to boys,
Zero restraint"; the other said, "I know."

I love you, Suzi, though the mouths repeat
Gross lies: as when a football team on tour
Rolls into town, the bus parks on your street
All afternoon; the other said, "I'm sure."
Cruel rumors, spread from the Dakotadome:
Ear to the phone, the other said, "She's home!"

PART TWO

23

I thought today when I came into work,
Luck filled the air; no heart could be appalled
On such a day, when coffee makers perk,
Virus detecting software all installed.
Except one friend of mine, I just found out—
Suddenly has to go, tomorrow night,
Up to Saint Matthew's, while I think about
Zappa long gone, though Betty Ford's all right.

I love you, Suzi, if today it's hard
Going through lists of all I need to do—
Reduced to nothing, every moment scarred,
And one love grows, without displacing you.
Call it bad luck, or does some other word
Evoke the coldness of what I've just heard?

24

If we could wave off bulletins of war,
Letting them slowly sink into the dirt,
Or, hypervigilant, each night watch more
Veiled slaves condemned to death over dessert—
Entirely opposite, this cruel news makes
Suzi's hair softer, her black eyes more kind.
Up from below, what has been sleeping wakes,
Zaftig, and longs to take her from behind.

I love you, Suzi. Though a sweet friend fights
Great danger, what I see most is your hair,
Rich in its color, throwing tiny lights
Around your face, and brightening the air.
Cold days have caught someone I love, but you,
Escaping for the moment, might pull through.

25

Ill and in danger, someone good and kind
Lies in the hospital, perhaps today.
Once more my thoughts are there. In Suzi's mind
Victims seem half a continent away.
Enter that white room, where the ceiling glows.
So strange, from here, to think of my friend's face
Up on the table, as the clean air flows,
Zinc tray, clamp, sterile cotton, all in place.

I love you Suzi. Lives are lived in round
Glandular worlds, defenseless on that day
Results come back all wrong from ultrasound
And on the film a light-blurred mass of gray,
Captured and occupied, kingdom of fear
(Except the odds get better every year).

26

It's strange to think of that one body part
Least capable of harm, at least not much.
Only three functions: nourishment to start,
Visual beauty, and the joy of touch.
Enough to think maybe they'd be exempt,
Safe in their classic line-drawn shape; not so:
Under the skin, as if in self-contempt,
Zapped by one errant photon, years ago.

I love you, Suzi. Maybe soon they'll make
Gold halter-tops as shields, where rays can't reach.
Ridiculous; what safety you can take
A joke, no more than sunscreen at the beach.
Cherish yourself, sweet Suzi, so you'll stay
Endlessly well, for guys who aren't half gay.

27

It's true that, underneath, all skin is bare.
Loose cotton blouses hide away so much.
One day I'd like to put my face in there,
Viewing what I can see but may not touch.
Enough of this. I think how bodies grow,
Safe, mostly, in prom dress and wedding gown,
Until, for reasons only demons know,
Zapped by a gene, they'll try to bring her down.

I love you, Suzi. Now my other friend
Gets better, slowly, and that's all I know.
Resting, she opens cards that people send,
And watches movies on the video.
Cheese casseroles, veal cutlets, chocolate cake
Enter her house, as rich as friends can make.

28

Thoughts on a Traveling Day

In Boston there's no Suzi; in Vermont
Loving her counts for nothing; she's at school,
On her computer—picks a cute, round font,
Verdana Bold, or maybe **Liverpool**.
End of a season. Where will Suzi be:
Safe in our town, or in another state,
Under a deadline, far away from me,
Zones that have been invisible of late?

I love you, Suzi. From this point in space
Gliding away from where my sick friend lies
Recovering, I think of your sweet face,
And how much I've been asked to subsidize.
Cool view from here; there's Cleveland on the lake—
Enough for me, but won't keep you awake.

29

I'm sitting at a talk on Robert Frost:
Low point, someone I love in jeopardy,
On wheeled beds, maybe now, taken and tossed,
Vast hallways toward the central surgery.
Embracing Suzi might help; I don't know:
Sent early in the day, I don't know where,
Under that round flood lamp where nurses go,
Zealously bright light falling through the air.

I love you, Suzi, more since my sweet friend
Got such bad luck I don't know what to say;
Riot of cells too small to comprehend,
Another caught—but cells don't think that way.
Cummings says this place stinks. He claims to know
Entry to a new universe. Let's go.

30

Thoughts While at a Conference

I have too many things to think about:
Loving someone in danger. First a talk
On "Light/Dark Imagery in Frost's 'Out, Out—'"
"Vermont as Canvas," then a pre-lunch walk.
Easy for me, as I don't need to face
Steel safety railings, on a high frame rolled
Up nurse-white halls, in that night-windowed place—
Zone where the light's so clean warm hands feel cold.

I love you, Suzi, though to be afraid
Goes nowhere; it's not me, only my friend
Rendered this helpless. Come, we've got it made:
And feeling good will help her, let's pretend.
Come sit with me, and let your perfect face
Erase all fear from its accustomed place.

31

I spent three days discussing Robert Frost,
Listened to lectures, most of which were good,
Only my heart was elsewhere, all but lost,
Vermont reduced to foliage and wood.
Easy for me to bear what each test gives.
She lies plain in the light, deep in a thin,
Utterly dark cave where a dragon lives,
Zinc scales, a riptooth of acetylene.

I love you, Suzi. All this scholar's tome
Goes to my friend, but also goes to you,
Resting late mornings in your trailer home,
A day with less than usual to do.
Calm thoughts, I've read, can help the blood create
Enzymes to let the cells recuperate.

32

I've looked at clouds from both sides, in a plane.
Landing, I've seen the hard ground speed and slow,
On this bright Sunday, flying back from Maine,
Vermont and Boston, as the strange thoughts flow.
Escape with me; we'll breathe the frost-hard air,
Sweet Suzi, if the cold days ever start,
Under a sky not wide enough to care,
Zero forgiveness, blood without a heart.

I love you, Suzi. I'll proclaim you can't
Get luck this bad, I hope. Just stick with me,
Resting together with a New Age chant
About the Gods our focus group can see
Cavorting mile-high, as this happy pair
Embrace, aloft, without a thing to wear.

33

Is It Appropriate to Indulge these Fantasies?

Incongruous at my age, but her face
Leads men to hazard pimples, or grow hair
On palms, dreaming of loose coils pinned in place,
Vamp-like, one spot behind her neck left bare.
Earth's oldest, cheapest date, but is this right?
Sometimes I know she's in some pickup truck.
Uneducated drivers, drunk each night,
Zoom through the back streets honking, flush with luck.

I love you, Suzi, though I haven't earned
Geishas *or* Ganymedes to buy drinks for.
Real girls are wonderful, but this year turned
All spoiled: my nephew dead, and now the war.
Can one go blind this late—or does that myth
Exist for those with dreams to go blind *with*?

Suzi as a Literary Object

It isn't hard to pull some famous verse—
Line, stanza, from the prompt-book in my head.
One scene, like Juliet freed from her nurse,
Viola out of drag and into bed.
Easy to add to this some mild complaint:
She smokes, she's friends with homophobic men.
Under it all, how good she looks in paint
(Zenith still droning on with CNN).

I love you, Suzi. If we'd been alive,
Growing and dying on that scepter'd isle
Ruled by Elizabeth, *then* I could swive
A girl with brown locks graced in Tudor style.
Come Suzi, watch me trim this goose's quill.
Each penstroke shows you dark and lovely still.

35

If Suzi's eyes could look more like the sun,
Lips red, or something near; her bare skin seen
Off-white, not much like snow, shield-factor one—
Vagrant soft hair—brown wires—what would that mean?
Each time I've brought her flowers I can see
Sun tones against her artificial tan.
Upwind, her Winston cloud drifts over me:
Zephyrs of blue smoke in a ceiling fan.

I love you, Suzi, thrill to hear your words.
Granted, it's not quite music, but who cares?
Running, ground level, sighing back at birds,
A mortal girl, on earth, as traffic stares.
Call me extreme, but Suzi in the sun
Exceeds all spreads that Hefner's ever run.

36

I won't admit some obstacle whose size,
Like baggage at the airport, slows us down,
Or makes me get discouraged if she buys
Vulgar wall paintings of a prairie town.
Enclosed at home, you must not drift away,
Seeing the hair go dull or firm breasts sag.
Until the red alert I pledge to stay
Zipped in together like a sleeping bag.

I love you, Suzi, even when your lips
Get wrinkled in the compass of time's blade,
Risking it all on monthly business trips,
Aware that when I'm gone more guys get laid.
Could I be wrong? If that's the charge they hurl,
Ed never wrote, and no man loved this girl.

37

In that time of the year when Suzi sees
Leaves hanging yellow from a branch half bare,
On days so warm even fox grapes won't freeze,
Vine-terraces like choir stalls lost in prayer.
End of the day; does Suzi see in me
Something alive, or something heading down
Under the darkened evening land, while she
Zeros my screen out and drives back to town?

I love you, Suzi. Think of me as coals
Gathered where we once lay in love (I wish).
Returning now, my shroud burned full of holes,
Aware I have no wine and just one fish.
Can these words function as a kind of text,
Each time you think about what happens next?

38

If she were in my class, I could spend years
Looking at Suzi's face while her black eyes
Open and look away, and in my ears
Voices tell me it's folly, waste, and lies.
Each day I've searched for some specific rule,
Studied the College Handbook, every part,
Unless I've missed the line: "Only a fool,
Zany, or clown lets such things even start."

I love you, Suzi. If the Handbook states
"Good teachers keep their eyes off girls this young—"
Roll up my office rug; a new job waits
At Monfort, where the fresh-killed steers are hung.
Casting cold eyes on what I long to do
Eases my collar-switch from white to blue.

39

The Fact That She is Less Than Half My Age

If I were less than twice as old as she,
Less than myself—would I then be enough
Of what she wants that she'd go out with me—
Vacation trips, or else just weekend stuff?
Easy to rant and rave and lose my breath.
So hard, sometimes, to keep her in my sight.
Up, down—the Buddha's wheel of birth and death
Zips out of all control, a tailless kite.

I love you Suzi, though the metaphor
Gets mixed up with itself, but I don't care—
Rolling my life's legs through your love-moon's door—
And makes a metric line that goes nowhere.
Cute, dark, breathtaking—and she's half my age.
Each man like me's just going through a stage.

40

It's weird to think—the day of Suzi's birth;
Less time from then to now than from the day
Of my first day to her first day on earth,
Voice shrill, ringing across the sixth of May.
Each time I count her decades, I say, "Well,
So what? She's not mine anyway to pick
Up in some dream world, where our shit won't smell,
Zones I can't even point to with a stick."

I love you, Suzi. Name what pleases you:
Good times, good trailer days, the Pageant prize.
Rakish in rented tux, I'll try to do
All that I can to brighten your black eyes:
Carbon-based gems that only pressure can
Encapsulate, just like on *Superman*.

Suzi Disguised as a Body Pillow

If lucky's what you call my life tonight,
Lucky I am; the figure in my bed,
On mattress springs, rests easy in my sight,
Vacantly stares, and lies back as if dead.
Erotic feelings come, but I do not.
Safe with soft cloth, no face, no neck, no arms,
Under the covers, warm but never hot,
Zoster no danger here, nor AIDS alarms.

I love you, Suzi. Though my words have been
Getting us nowhere, still I feel I've wed
Round-featured warmth, the touch of cloth on skin,
And afterward, no ashtray in the bed,
Classic, strong legs, with nothing in between,
Easy to talk to, and a cinch to clean.

42

On the Campus Walkway

It's light that does it, more than anything;
Light makes a shape come clear, keeps faces warm
On summer session days that always bring
Vague breezes through the window of a dorm.
Easy to look at her brown hair all day,
Strolling along the paved paths in the sun,
Unsweating, slowly, on the dry walkway;
Zoology—she's late but does not run.

I love you, Suzi. And I love to stare
Gently into a real man's favorite place.
Rushmore-bound tourist buses speed to where
All will see Lincoln, none the state's best face,
Clear in the sun, above the dry asphalt
Edged with remains of last year's safety salt.

Suzi Drinking Soda on a Hot Day

I wish I had the skill to frame her face:
Lips ringed around an ice-cold Royal Crown
On days so hot the trained greyhounds won't chase
Valley Park's rabbit, so the track shuts down.
End of the summer; Suzi takes the sun,
Sun touches Suzi. Next week every hall
Up in our building will see people run,
Zipping up stairways, meaning now it's fall.

I love you, Suzi. When you lift that clear
Glass bottle to your lips, and swirl the dark
Raspberry-flavored cola-spiked root beer
Around your mouth—the world's a water park,
Crowded with swimmers drinking Mountain Dew.
Each bottle, spun, finds north, and points to you.

44

It almost looked as if she was asleep,
Loose-jointed, not quite seeing where she went,
Outside a bar where students crowd like sheep,
Voices cranked high in their close element.
Easy for me to laugh, but there's a way
Some people walk that makes me love this town,
Under beige overcast, the round-edged way
Zinc vapor lamps project what's bounced back down.

I love you, Suzi, striding bar to bar.
Go party on the town; tonight you're free.
Rip thorns from bushes; scratch your boyfriend's car,
And if he finds out, tell him it was me
Carrying branches for a lumber drive
Established when Paul Bunyan was alive.

45

In all the pictures that I have of her
Lodged in my mind, I can't quite fix my gaze
On any storm-front color, just a blur,
Vast as the range where Monfort cattle graze.
End of the day; a certain light slants past,
Shines in her trailer, loud with MTV.
Up north, folks with camcorders drive too fast,
Zoom lenses set for twisters they won't see.

I love you, Suzi. When a front moves in,
Gold shines behind the thunderheads, when trash
Rolls up and down your street, wind shakes the tin
Around your window, and a blue-black flash
Cuts power—don't get brave and run outside
Euphoric, like that girl last year who died.

46

Suzi as a Nonexistent Person

I dream sometimes I'm in a Key West bar,
Locked in the bathroom. Do I dare to drive?
Outside, the show goes on, the lip-synch star
Voicelessly belting out "I Will Survive."
Each time I think of Suzi, it's as if
Spring never happened, summer just a joke
Unfolding in a sandbox, like a whiff,
Zephyr, mistral, or just her Winston smoke.

I love you, Suzi, though you seem to be
Gone from the world, a body pillow held,
Removed as far from cold reality
As those who railed at Franklin "Rosenfeld."
Come back from nothing, let your soft brown hair
Erase the fact that you're not really there.

Some Linguistic Theories

In S.I. Hayakawa's book he states:
Language is why our mouths evolved this way.
Once I had felt how soft a wet tongue skates,
Velvet on skin—that's not what I would say.
Ears come alive when licked, a flushed birthmark,
Skin cooled with moisture quickens in the air,
Under the floodlights of her trailer park,
Zoned so you can't plant flowers anywhere.

I love you, Suzi. My hypothesis
Goes this way: Tongues evolved for our delight.
Rare chance for me, but someone's mouth will kiss
All parts of you, both mouths awake all night.
Chomsky says no: Grammar creates the thought,
Except in Pyongyang, where pure truth is taught.

48

An Apologetically Sexist Meditation in Time of War

I've seen how cars with flags will surge ahead,
Lurch to a stop, then screech their tires again.
On North Street, engines race, to mask the dead
Voiceover on the air from CNN.
Everyone's edgy in a war, of course.
Still, I can love this day: how light hangs hard
Under a sky of overwhelming force,
Zones paced off by the Regional Air Guard.

I love you, Suzi. If I wore four stars,
Girls too could have their finest hour: dress sleek,
Respect the officers you meet in bars,
And sleep with one enlisted man each week.
Can this be right, or just that famous lie
Explaining how it's dignified to die?

Her Possible Fiancé

"I really need some help here," Suzi said,
Late Sunday night over the telephone;
"Or else I'll have to live on Wonder Bread,
Vanilla squares, or rice and beans alone."
Each day, almost, I see her with the man
She swears is not a homophobic ape.
(Unschooled, he says Mormon electrodes can
Zap one's arousal patterns back to shape.)

I love you, Suzi. If this man you see
Gives you as much as I, or even less,
Run to his arms. When he says, "Marry me,"
All your sweet voice should go to saying "Yes!"
Call out the bride with Lohengrin's first bars;
Eros lives here among the lawn-parked cars.

PART THREE

50

The Difference Between Suzi's Boyfriends and Me

In dark times, months when clams are safe to eat,
Let me be sure of what I value most,
Of what I hope for, as the rising heat
Vetoes December up the Middle Coast.
Endlessly weird to think of her with guys;
Strange that they could find things to say to her,
Until once more the capillaries rise,
Zoology-controlled, and she a blur.

I love you, Suzi. When some baseball hat
Gets you in bed, he'll know he's with warm skin.
Reaching that same place, I'll know more than that,
And realize I'm with Suzi, slipping in
Clean sheets at Super 8, where V. Patel
Emerges smiling at the check-in bell.

51

Suzi Tells a Lie

I called; she promised she'd give me a buzz
Later, after her study group, she said …
Offhand I wondered what the topic was.
"Van Gogh," she answered, and the line went dead.
Easy to take her at her word, but still,
Students in her department never take
Ungraded things like Flemish Art to fill
Zero-sum schedules that might not make.

I love you, Suzi, though the things you said
Gave me more proof that what I need's not there.
Reading Mark Doty's book, I lay in bed
And wondered, as in pop songs, "Where oh where
Can Suzi be, and is that class a fake?"
(Easily solved, but not when wide awake.)

52

In dark times, when my mind begins to see
Love as an empty field lit by black eyes,
Old dreams of what I've lost come back to me:
Visions of Suzi taking on five guys.
Erase the notions; nothing holds them up,
Save for one flash of Suzi on her dates,
Unzipped, down to a thong and a C cup,
Zinc bracelet ringing, as her boyfriend waits.

I love you, Suzi, even though I threw
Gold after you for nothing; I don't care.
Real girls are better in the sheets, but you
Are better still, since you lie everywhere,
Chatting into the phone, a fantasy
Each man born normal gets to touch; not me.

53

In dark times, when my mind begins to see
Lost chances, like the time when she walked past
Outdoors; I could have told her, "Come with me;
Vermillion beer is cold, but warms up fast."
Email is useless, I don't even know
Suzi's address, if she's online at all.
Until she calls me back, I'll have to go
Zigzagging post to pillar, stairs to hall.

I love you, Suzi, even as the fact
Grows in its hardness, that you hold no hope:
Real, ruthless as the Cheney-Rhenquist pact,
And wasteful as the years when I did dope.
Cold fills my chest to think it: that we might
End up as ships that go bump in the night.

54

I'm trying to compare two faces. One
Looks just like Suzi, in a beat-up Dodge.
Off to the other side, a shape to stun
Viewers who get to see her décolletage.
Easily moving through the bar's close press,
She backed against me; I could smell her hair,
Unfastened, and her flesh filled out her dress—
Zaftig, I guess you'd say, if that word's fair.

I love you, Suzi. That will stay the same.
Girls may appear, so cute I stagger home,
Renee especially, even her name:
A touch as soft as how some styling foam
Cools down on contact in a mirrored bath
Edged in the bronze that moved the ox to Rath.

55

Suzi Smoking

It's worst of all her habits, that I'm sure,
Learned from Joe Camel, with his pool-cue set,
On those days when she leans back in the pure
Vapor that spreads out from her cigarette
(Emblem of all I hope she'll leave behind;
Southern Republicans gain with each pack,
Up where soft money campaign checks are signed,
Zillions in banks—more die from this than crack).

I love you, Suzi. If you want to smoke,
Go right ahead; you're not my employee.
Real men, inside real pickup trucks, will joke
About that queer you sometimes design to see.
Camels, or Camel Filters: I don't care.
Each pack hides Suzi's face in Old Joe's hair.

56

If lately Suzi hasn't called to say,
"Listen; I really need some help from you,"
Old tunes don't fade; she'll call by Saturday,
Voice musical and soft. Guess what I'll do?
Electric bills have shocked her; Great Plains Gas
Smothers her on her bill-strewn study space,
Under a swag lamp with a chain of brass:
Zero zero one two—she rings my place.

I love you, Suzi. Every time I mend
Gaps in your funds, I love you even more.
Riffle through bills the Visa people send,
And find yourself at my apartment door.
"Come in," I'll say. But you'll just use the john,
Explaining that you've left the car turned on.

57

I've never been a banker; if I were
Loans would flow first to girls with soft brown hair,
Old funds to young; maybe I'd buy her fur,
Vacation with her in the desert air.
Each day I think how deeply in the red
She's fallen; every week adds one percent,
Until the time we put this debt to bed,
Zip bags together like a silken tent.

I love you, Suzi; I can't wish away
Great sums like this; let's try to strike a deal.
Relax with me, my girlfriend for a day,
And see if we can make each other feel
Comfort with budgets, on one thrifty night,
Erased in one stroke—or is that not right?

58

How Can I Adjust a Debt and Not Make Suzi Look Bad?

If I should say her debts could disappear,
Loans cancelled with a word—that isn't quite
On target, though I know she wants to hear
Verbal assurance that I'll make things right.
Erase the figures, amortize the book;
Suzi can pay with nothing, half, or more.
Unfair perhaps, how that would make her look:
Zero in debt, but gave away the store.

I love you, Suzi. Speak and it's a deal:
Great plans: a film, a Chinese take-out, then,
Returning to your mobile home, our meal,
Almond Mu Shu; we're hungry once again.
Citibank never works like this; a debt
Ends up sold for whatever they can get.

59

Suzi Getting Ready for the State Beauty Pageant

Indigo fringe—or maybe that's too much—
Lips glossed to catch the television light.
Over it all, foundation, just a touch,
Vanilla-colored, verging toward off-white.
Experimenting in her trailer, sun
Slices through blinds as she holds still to check
Under her chin for places not yet done:
Zits, hairs—then smoothes it farther down her neck.

I love you, Suzi. I can't wait to see
Gold brushed across your cheeks, the clearly lined
Rim of your mouth (that's never once touched me),
And eyes on stage—indelibly designed,
Contoured face surfaces; please let me just
Enjoy a touch of it before we're dust.

Fall Colors, Beauty Pageant

I've never seen a face matched with the fall
Like Suzi's. Leaves give off a final heat
Of yellow-shifted sun, and nearly all
Vermillion rustles through them with their feet.
Elsewhere, a hundred beauties will convene—
Some Radisson in Pierre, fixed frontier style.
Up on the stage, culled down to seventeen,
Zapped by the cameras' flash, they smile and smile.

I love you, Suzi. When this light comes down,
Goes pale and yellow, I can trace your life,
Raised in the flat land—as the leaves go brown,
And envelopes are opened with a knife,
Crisply, till one last pair of painted eyes
Ends bathed in light, and everybody cries.

61

I want to see her there, in wax-bright lips,
Long fall raised high, that dark facsimile
Of hair held tight in alligator clips.
Vine-like, some strands hang down as if pulled free.
End of the pageant; Sara Frankenstein
Steps down, and takes her monstrous name away.
Up near the podium they stand in line,
Zipped tight in gowns, rehearsing what they'll say.

I love you, Suzi, and I want to be
Good friend to Miss Clay County, this sweet girl,
Resting backstage with ashtray on her knee
And more hair falling loose from morning's curl.
Corny, I know, but Suzi's on the stage,
Exactly marketed for men my age.

62

Imagining the way she looks up there,
Lights warm against her skin, I see her stand
On risers, in a crowd of floodlit hair,
Votes tallied, and the envelope in hand.
Each fall they seek the pageant's golden fleece,
Show off school monologues, to parents' cheers,
Until that moment (Bert Parks, rest in peace)
Zoom lenses rush to show the winner's tears.

I love you, Suzi. You deserve it all.
Go forward on the stage in your high heels.
Remember that there sits in this large hall
A man who knows how wanting something feels.
Can she not win? She claimed it was a fix:
Ethnicity controlled the final picks.

63

On the Day of the University Parade

I looked for her on floats, and on the street.
Lagging behind, I saw through crowded blur
One girl, with raised-heel sandals on her feet,
Very like Suzi, but it wasn't her.
Each float that passed, each high school marching band,
Stood waiting at parade rest in the road,
Until someone on the reviewing stand
(Zeus on Olympus), flashed the score in code.

I love you, Suzi. No doubt you were there,
Gawking at antique cars, your current date
Resting his right hand on your soft brown hair,
And with his left—well, that's the thing I hate.
Crisp drums rang through the air, autumnal sound
Ending at last, and Suzi not around.

64

Thinking about Suzi on a Day When I Don't Have Any Desire For Her

It doesn't matter. Even if I can't
Lustily take her, in her boyfriends' way,
Or bulge beneath my denim pants and pant
Voraciously, I still feel good today.
Even if she's not at the fall parade,
Sex as a concept fills the leaf-blown air,
Up in the ozone where the contrails fade,
Zero degrees, a freezer vault up there.

I love you, Suzi. These are normal scenes.
Grown men must pace themselves, most doctors say.
Rest for a week, eat oysters, liver, greens,
(And don't touch boys); just think of her each day,
Cool in her dress, beyond all pelvic ache.
Each man my age will sometimes need a break.

In a College Bar on Halloween

I like to think of Suzi on this night,
Leaving her trailer, in a dress she sewed,
On this rare time when girls in college might
Venture beyond their casual dress code.
Exotic dancers, sexy vampires, whores—
So different now, skin painted, in the dark.
Under a roof that screens a tavern's doors
Zircon tiaras flash with icy spark.

I love you, Suzi, sight for weary eyes.
Girls have been bagged in shapeless cloth all year,
Returning Monday to the somber dyes
And denims of November's cold career.
Corpses must show ID for drinks. No doubt
Each wax-pale face is checking Suzi out.

Watching Suzi Pull Out of my Driveway

I like the way her red car lights the bare
Leaf cover, as she turns and waves to me,
Or maybe she just flicks a bit of hair
Vaguely out of her eyes so she can see.
Each day just hangs there, tries to rain, and fails.
Seeding the clouds might help, or maybe not.
Under a sky made up of vapor trails
Zones of high pressure show the earth's too hot.

I love you, Suzi—how your traced eyelids
Go with the hectic shades fall's famous for:
Red, yellow, trick-or-treating high school kids
Arriving, cigarette-breathed, at my door.
Chilly companion, as you drive away,
Each leaf-gust says I've lost another day.

67

Watching Suzi Drive Away on a Day When She Looks Heavier

> *My daughter's heavier. Light leaves are flying.*
> John Berryman, *The Dream Songs*, #385

Is Suzi gaining weight? The falling leaves
Look like Thanksgiving birds lined up to die,
Or flocks of chickens hiding under eaves,
Victim of feather-shears so they can't fly.
Each fall sticks farther back into my throat.
Sundays are worst: thoughts of my other friend
Unsaddled hard, then waving from the float,
Zipped in a robe to let her right arm bend.

I love you, Suzi. These brown times of year
Give strength, if this heat cools, for us to face
Rent hikes imposed on sound frame houses here.
(Absurd to think I'm younger than this place.)
Coasting to turn, she joins the traffic flow
East on West North, where I don't like to go.

About the Author

Ed Allen has authored two novels, *Straight Through the Night* and *Mustang Sally*, as well as the story collection *Ate It Anyway*, which received the Flannery O'Connor Award for Short Fiction in 2003. *Mustang Sally* was made into a film, *Easy Six*, for Showtime in 2005. A former three-day contestant on *Jeopardy*, Allen is an associate professor of English at the University of South Dakota.

Ahsahta Press

SAWTOOTH POETRY PRIZE SERIES

2002: AARON MCCOLLOUGH, *Welkin* (Brenda Hillman, judge)
2003: GRAHAM FOUST, *Leave the Room to Itself* (Joe Wenderoth, judge)
2004: NOAH ELI GORDON, *The Area of Sound Called the Subtone* (Claudia Rankine, judge)
2005: KARLA KELSEY, *Knowledge, Forms, the Aviary* (Carolyn Forché, judge)

NEW SERIES

ED ALLEN, *67 Mixed Messages*
DAN BEACHY-QUICK, *Spell*
BRIGITTE BYRD, *Fence Above the Sea*
LISA FISHMAN, *Dear, Read*
PEGGY HAMILTON, *Forbidden City*
CHARLES O. HARTMAN, *Island*
SANDRA MILLER, *Oriflamme*
ETHAN PAQUIN, *The Violence*
LANCE PHILLIPS, *Corpus Socius*
LANCE PHILLIPS, *Cur aliquid vidi*
HEATHER SELLERS, *Drinking Girls and Their Dresses*
LIZ WALDNER, *Saving the Appearances*

MODERN AND CONTEMPORARY POETRY OF THE AMERICAN WEST

SANDRA ALCOSSER, *A Fish to Feed All Hunger*
DAVID AXELROD, *Jerusalem of Grass*
DAVID BAKER, *Laws of the Land*
DICK BARNES, *Few and Far Between*
CONGER BEASELEY, JR., *Over DeSoto's Bones*

LINDA BIERDS, *Flights of the Harvest-Mare*
RICHARD BLESSING, *Winter Constellations*
BOYER, BURMASTER, AND TRUSKY, EDS., *The Ahsahta Anthology*
PEGGY POND CHURCH, *New and Selected Poems*
KATHARINE COLES, *The One Right Touch*
WYN COOPER, *The Country of Here Below*
CRAIG COTTER, *Chopstix Numbers*
JUDSON CREWS, *The Clock of Moss*
H.L. DAVIS, *Selected Poems*
SUSAN STRAYER DEAL, *The Dark is a Door*
SUSAN STRAYER DEAL, *No Moving Parts*
LINDA DYER, *Fictional Teeth*
GRETEL EHRLICH, *To Touch the Water*
GARY ESAREY, *How Crows Talk and Willows Walk*
JULIE FAY, *Portraits of Women*
THOMAS HORNSBY FERRIL, *Anvil of Roses*
THOMAS HORNSBY FERRIL, *Westering*
HILDEGARDE FLANNER, *The Hearkening Eye*
CHARLEY JOHN GREASYBEAR, *Songs*
CORRINNE HALES, *Underground*
HAZEL HALL, *Selected Poems*
NAN HANNON, *Sky River*
GWENDOLEN HASTE, *Selected Poems*
KEVIN HEARLE, *Each Thing We Know Is Changed Because We Know It And Other Poems*
SONYA HESS, *Kingdom of Lost Waters*
CYNTHIA HOGUE, *The Woman in Red*
ROBERT KRIEGER, *Headlands, Rising*
ELIO EMILIANO LIGI, *Disturbances*
HANIEL LONG, *My Seasons*
KEN MCCULLOUGH, *Sycamore•Oriole*
NORMAN MCLEOD, *Selected Poems*
BARBARA MEYN, *The Abalone Heart*
DAVID MUTSCHLECNER, *Esse*
DIXIE PARTRIDGE, *Deer in the Haystacks*
GERRYE PAYNE, *The Year-God*

GEORGE PERREAULT, *Curved Like an Eye*
HOWARD W. ROBERTSON, *to the fierce guard in the Assyrian Saloon*
LEO ROMERO, *Agua Negra*
LEO ROMERO, *Going Home Away Indian*
MIRIAM SAGAN, *The Widow's Coat*
PHILIP ST. CLAIR, *At the Tent of Heaven*
PHILIP ST. CLAIR, *Little-Dog-of-Iron*
DONALD SCHENKER, *Up Here*
GARY SHORT, *Theory of Twilight*
D.J. SMITH, *Prayers for the Dead Ventriloquist*
RICHARD SPEAKES, *Hannah's Travel*
GENEVIEVE TAGGARD, *To the Natural World*
TOM TRUSKY, ED., *Women Poets of the West*
MARNIE WALSH, *A Taste of the Knife*
BILL WITHERUP, *Men at Work*
CAROLYNE WRIGHT, *Stealing the Children*

This book is set in Apollo type
with Helvetica Neue Condensed Bold titles
and Helvetica Neue 75 Bold numbers
by Ahsahta Press at Boise State University
and manufactured on acid-free paper
by Boise State University Printing and Graphics, Boise, Idaho.
Cover design by Grant Olsen and Janet Holmes.

AHSAHTA PRESS
2006

JANET HOLMES, DIRECTOR

AMY GARRETT-BROWN
ABSOLOM J. HAGG
MICHAELA HERLIHY
ADRIAN T. KIEN
TIMOTHY D. ORME
AMY WEGNER, INTERN
ABIGAIL L. WOLFORD